ESCAPE ROOM PUZZLES
ECO DOME DISASTER

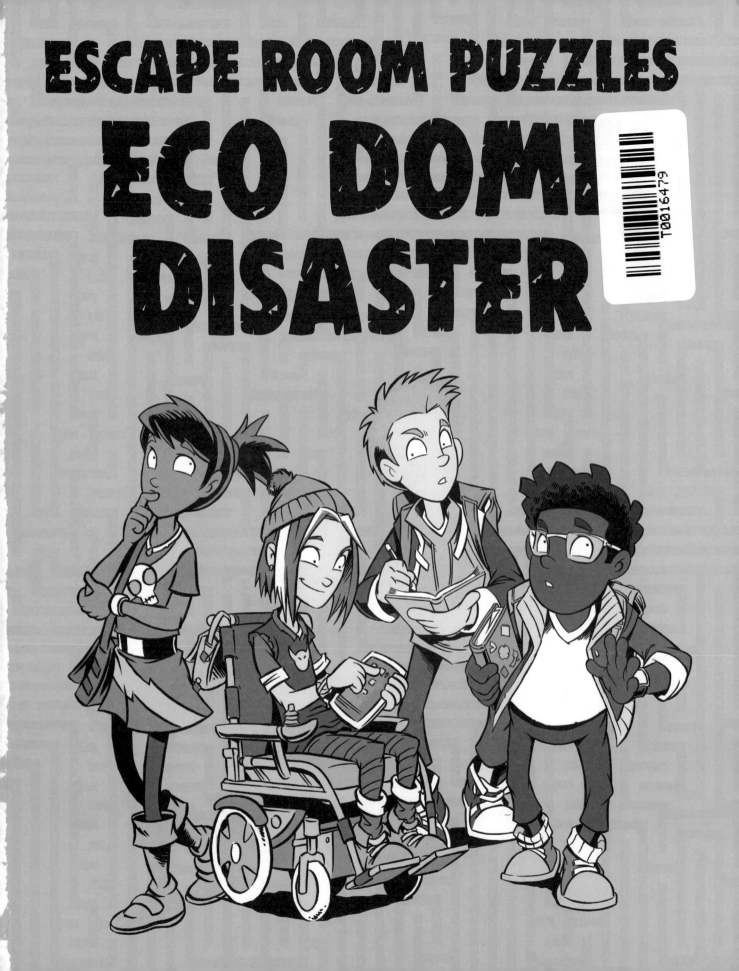

KINGFISHER
LONDON & NEW YORK

Copyright © Macmillan Publishers
International Ltd 2022
First published in 2022 by Kingfisher,
120 Broadway, New York, NY 10271
Kingfisher is an imprint of Macmillan
Children's Books, London
All rights reserved.

Distributed in the U.S. and Canada
by Macmillan, 120 Broadway,
New York, NY 10271

EU representative: Macmillan Publishers Ireland
Ltd, 1st Floor, The Liffey Trust Centre, 117-126
Sheriff Street Upper, Dublin 1, D01 YC43

Library of Congress
Cataloging-in-Publication
data has been applied for.

Written, designed, and illustrated
by Dynamo Limited

ISBN: 978-0-7534-7838-7

Kingfisher books are available for
special promotions and premiums.
For details contact: Special Markets
Department, Macmillan, 120 Broadway,
New York, NY 10271.

For more information, please visit
www.kingfisherbooks.com

Printed in China
9 8 7 6 5 4 3 2 1
1TR/0522/RV/WKT/120WF

ESCAPE ROOM PUZZLES
ECO DOME DISASTER

KINGFISHER
LONDON & NEW YORK

CONTENTS

MEET THE TEAM!

Hey! I'm Kiran.

Ethan here!

NAME: Kiran

STRENGTHS: Leader and organizer

FUN FACT: Loves extreme sports—especially rock climbing

NAME: Ethan

STRENGTHS: Math and science genius

FUN FACT: Amazing memory for facts and always wins any quiz

Hello! Zane's the name.

Hi!

NAME: Zane

STRENGTHS: Creative and thinks outside the box

FUN FACT: Loves art and takes his trusty sketchbook wherever he goes

NAME: Cassia

STRENGTHS: Technology pro

FUN FACT: Queen of gadgets and invents her own apps

WELCOME!

Kiran, Ethan, Cassia, and Zane are on the trail of another exciting adventure, but what have they got mixed up in *this* time?

The awesome foursome are on a school science trip to an eco dome filled with exotic plants from around the world. The dome is famous for its research into rare and endangered plant species—and that's where the trouble starts ...

When Kiran spots a trail of green slime oozing from under the door in the entrance lobby, she decides to investigate, closely followed by the rest of the gang! They soon find themselves tracking the toxic trail through an underground network of tunnels and laboratories, deeper and deeper into the heart of the building... and deeper into danger.

YOUR MISSION:
You must find the source of the toxic slime and neutralize it before it can escape into the outside world, spread out of control, and cause an eco-disaster!

WHAT YOU NEED TO KNOW:

- Each laboratory studies different rare and often dangerous species. Do NOT underestimate the plant life!

- The labs and corridors are protected by fiendish security systems—so you'll need to be on your guard!

- The slime trail is doubling in size every 30 minutes. In only a few hours, it will burst out of the building—and then there'll be no stopping it!

Don't forget!

You must look out for six leaf symbols as you move through the building. You'll need to collect them all to complete your mission.

ROOM ONE:
THE ECO DOME

Welcome to the Crystal Geode—a world-famous eco dome devoted to rare and exotic plants from all over the planet. This is going to be one awesome school trip!

As the teacher hands out maps of the dome to the class, Kiran notices a strange green light shining from under a doorway marked "PRIVATE". Quickly, she signals to the rest of the gang to take a look. "What's that?" she whispers.

You all sneak forward to take a closer look and a blob of green slime slowly oozes out from under the door. It's time to investigate. Kiran turns the handle of the door and you all step inside. YUCK! What's that terrible smell? It's a cross between rotting cabbage and bad eggs! You're all so busy trying to hold your noses that no one notices the door swing shut. The door locks with a loud click and you find yourselves trapped in a white lobby splattered with glowing (not to mention foul-smelling!) green slime. But how did it get here?

COLOR WALL

Ethan sheepishly pokes a blob of the slime with his map and to his surprise, it lets out a hissing sound! It quickly bubbles up and melts the edge of the map. This stuff must be toxic, so whatever you do, don't touch it! The glowing trail disappears under a door ahead marked "RESTRICTED ACCESS." In the middle of the door is a touch screen with a patterned wall on it. Your task is to identify the correct missing piece to complete the wall and open the door.

◊ ECO FACT

Scientists have only studied a fraction of the existing known plant species on Earth, but of those that have been examined, over two-thirds face extinction in the not-too-distant future.

1

2

It looks like we need to match up the colors!

Don't rush! We may only get one chance at this!

3

Perfect fit!

You identify the correct piece with no problems. Ethan presses it and the door slides open ...

11

MATRIX MIX UP

Up ahead, you can just make out a long corridor. It leads down into darkness and is covered in a glowing green trail of slime, which seems to have taken out the lights! Cassia quickly hacks into the dome's lighting system with her tablet, and a matrix of zeros appears on screen. There must be some faulty connections in there somewhere, but Cassia can fix them ... if she can find them!

Can you help her identify the faulty connections? You are looking for five symbols in the matrix that are different from all the others.

Hey, check out that leaf symbol! I'm going to draw it in my sketch pad! It might come in handy.

```
OOOOOOOOOOOOOO
OOOOOOOOOOOOOO
OOOOOOOOOOOOOO
OOOOOOOOOOOOOO
OOOOOOOOOOOOOO
OOOOOODOOOOOO
OOOOOOOOOOOOOO
OOOOOOOOOOOOOO
OOOOOOOOOOOOOO
OOOOOOOOOOOOOO
OOOOOOOOOOOOOO
OOOOOOOOOOOOOO
OOOOOOOOOOOOOO
OOOOOOOOOOOOOO
OOOOOOOOOOOOOO
OOOOOOOOOOOOOO
OOOOOOOOOOOOOO
OOOOOOOOOOOOOO
OOOOOOOOOOOOOO
OOOOOOOOOOOOOO
OOOOOOOOOOOOOO
OOOOOOOOOOOOOO
```

This is pretty tricky!

```
OOOOOOOOOOOOOOOOOOOOOOOOOOOOOOOOOOOOOOO
OOOOOOOOOOOOOOOOOOOOOOOOOOOOOOOOOOOOOO
OOOOOOOPOOOOOOOOOOOOOOOOOOOOOOOOOOOOOO
OOOOOOOOOOOOOOOOOOOOOOOOOOOOOOOOOOOOOO
OOOOOOOOOOOOOOOOOOOOOOOOOOOOOOOOOOOOOO
OOOOOOOOOOOOOOOOOOOOOOOOOOOOOOOOOOOOOO
OOOOOOOOOOOOOOOOOOOOOUOOOOOOOOOOOOOOOO
OOOOOOOOOOOOOOOOOOOOOOOOOOOOOOOOOOOOOO
OOOOOOOOOOOOOOOOOOOOOOOOOOOOOOOOOOOOOO
OOOOOOOOOOOOOOOOUOOOOOOOOOOOOOOOOOOOOO
OOOOOOOOOOOOOOOOOOOOOOOOOOOOOOOOOOOOOO
OOOOOOOOOOOOOOOOOOOOOOOOOOOOOOOOOOOOOO
OOOOOOOOOOOOOOOOOOOOOOOOOOOOOOOOOOOOOO
OOOOOOOOOOOOOOOOOOOOOOOOOOOOOOOOOOOOOO
OOOOOOOOOOOOOOOOOOOOOOOOOOOOOOOOCOOOOO
OOOOOOOOOOOOOOOOOOOOOOOOOOOOOOOOOOOOOO
OOOOOOOOOOOOOOOOOOOOOOOOOOOOOOOOOOOOOO
OOOOOOGOOOOOOOOOOOOOOOOOOOOOOOOOOOOOOOO
OOOOOOOOOOOOOOOOOOOOOOOOOOO
OOOOOOOOOOOOOOOOOOOOOOOOOO
OOOOOOOOOOOOOOOOOOOOOOOOO
OOOOOOOOOOOOOOOOOOOOOOO
```

Eagle eye!

As soon as Cassia clicks on the last symbol, the lights come back on with a flash. It's time to head on down the corridor, following the trail of slime …

THE KEY TO FREEDOM?

At the end of the corridor, you find yourselves in a square hallway with locked doors on every wall and green slime dripping everywhere! Ethan checks what remains of his map of the dome. You are now in the storage area. If you can find the way out, it will lead you to the research labs. Luckily, you find a key on the floor—but it can only open ONE locked door.
Which door should you open to find your way out?

ECO FACT

Most plants feed by taking up water and minerals through their roots, but carnivorous plants, such as the Venus flytrap, attract then digest insects. Some species even dine on small rodents and lizards!

Free at last!

You made it out! Ahead is a large sign saying "RESEARCH ROOM," and a long trail of green ooze. It's time to move on to the next part of your adventure ...

ROOM TWO: THE RESEARCH ROOM

As you enter the Research Room, you look around in awe. It feels like you are walking into a lively rain forest. All around you there are giant plants, tangled vines, and huge, colorful flowers you've never seen before. Strangely, though, the place seems to be deserted ...

Even more worrying, the slime trail appears to be taking over in here! Most of the plants are covered with the weird green goo, and the air is filled with a nasty odour of rotten eggs and cabbage.

"We have to find out where that stuff is coming from—and quick," says Kiran. "It could kill these plants if we don't stop it!" There's not a moment to waste, so the team quickly gets to work.

FEED ME!

You all follow the trail of slime through a pair of enormous glass doors into the biggest greenhouse you've ever seen—but there's no one around. In front of you is a huge trough housing five strange-looking plants. Next to it there's a locked cabinet and a large sign. As Kiran carefully studies the sign, you realize that you'll need to get into the cabinet.

TOP SECRET
GROWTH EXPERIMENT

All seedlings MUST be fed at 10:00 am every day. Failure to do so will void results.

Mix each tub of plant food with exactly six cups of water and pour over the roots of each plant.

It's nearly 10 o'clock. We can't let the experiment fail! I bet the plant food is kept in the locked cabinet.

Can you figure out the missing digits on the cabinet code pad to open it? It looks like the outside numbers relate to the inside number somehow ...

Hint
Experiment with different sums using the numbers on the outside of one triangle!

I think each triangle follows the same pattern!

Summed up!
You type in the missing digits and the cabinet clicks open. Sure enough, there are five tubs of plant food inside with writing on them ...

MATCH UP

Now that the cabinet is unlocked, you need to work out which tub of food is for each plant—but it's not going to be easy. There are only pictures of the fruit on the labels—and the plants themselves all look very similar! Can you decipher which food belongs to which plant using the information on the labels?

Giant prickly paw

Red petals
5 petals
Orange center
Long stem
Leaves in groups of 3

PLANT NUMBER:

Spiky neon nut

Orange petals
4 petals
Red center
2 stems
Leaves in pairs

PLANT NUMBER:

Thorny devil fruit

Red petals
4 petals
Orange center
Short stem
Leaves in groups of 3

PLANT NUMBER:

Ghost fingers

Orange petals
4 petals
Red center
3 stems
Leaves in pairs

PLANT NUMBER:

Bristling bananas

Red petals
4 petals
Orange center
Long stem
Leaves in groups of 3

PLANT NUMBER:

Expert identifying!

Now you know which plant
is which, but you're not done
with the task just yet!
There's still work to do ...

CUP CONUNDRUM

Before you can feed the plants, you must mix the food for each one with exactly 6 cups of water. In the cabinet there are also two vessels. One holds 9 cups of water, the other holds 4 cups. Can you determine how to measure out 6 cups of water? It's a tricky problem, but luckily there is space in Zane's sketchbook to do some figuring out.

CAPACITY:
9 CUPS

CAPACITY:
4 CUPS

⬥ ECO FACT

One desert plant, nicknamed the resurrection plant, can survive for years without water. It curls up into a dried out ball, but opens in just a few hours when it comes into contact with water again.

Hint

You can empty and refill the cups as many times as you need.

Work out your answer here!

Hunger satisfied!

At last, the team can feed the plants and the experiment is saved! It's time to head deeper into the greenhouse on the trail of the glowing goo ...

SUPER STING!

You gaze around the greenhouse in utter amazement—this place is incredible! Suddenly an alarm sounds and the doors swing shut. Before you even have time to think, a hatch in the ceiling opens and a swarm of giant insects flies in, ready to pollinate the flowers.

Yikes! The swarm buzzes angrily around your heads—and some of those monsters have stingers. But don't panic, you can catch them with nets! You'll need to net every last one with a stinger if you want to escape without getting a super-sized jab. Can you catch all 10 of them?

Phew!

That was a close call! At last,
the swarm is under control
and you can keep following
the slime trail. But where
will it lead you next?

ROOM THREE: CARNIVOROUS ZONE

Awesome work, team! You've helped with a top-secret experiment and even managed to escape from a swarm of giant insects. If you can do that, tracking down the source of a little green slime should be a cinch! But don't relax just yet ... the dome's research center is huge. You're yet to find the missing researchers and who knows what other weird plants are lurking down here?

You won't have to wait long to find out! The team is now entering the Carnivorous Zone—home to some monster-sized plants with an appetite to match. Just like the greenhouse, this place is deserted apart from the scary-looking plant life, of course. And boy, is it humid in here! So wipe the sweat from your forehead and keep your concentration. It's time for the next challenge.

SWEET DREAMS!

There's green slime everywhere in this room! It's even smothering some of the monster plants—and they don't look happy about it. In fact, it looks like the toxic goo is burning their leaves! You need to clean it off at once, but that may be easier said than done. On the wall there is a big warning sign but it appears to be obstructed by some green goo. You all move in cautiously for a closer look.

The bottom-left digit of the code has been obliterated by green goo. Can you work out what it is?

DANGER
FLESH-EATING PLANTS!

Do not approach or handle plants unless they are sleeping.

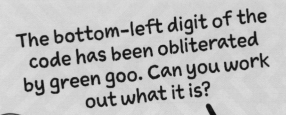

PIPE PUZZLE

Now what? Those hungry plants might be falling asleep, but how are you going to clean off all that goo? Suddenly, Cassia has a brainwave. She can hack into the dome's central control system and turn on the water sprinklers remotely. That should do the trick! Cassia quickly enters some lines of code into her tablet and a map of the sprinkler system appears on screen. But which water hose supplies the Carnivorous Zone?

Ha! Ha! Ha!

What did the Venus flytrap say to the waiter in the restaurant?

I'll have a burger with flies!

🌿 ECO FACT

Borneo's *Nepenthes rajah* is the biggest carnivorous plant in the world. Its urn-shaped traps can grow up to 16 inches (41 centimeters) tall and hold nearly a gallon (3.5 liters) of water.

Nice work!

Cassia selects the hose and the sprinklers begin to spray water over the plants, washing away the green goo. It looks like your work in here is done ... or is it?

TOXIC LAKE

The plants might be getting a wash, but the lab floor is quickly filling up with puddles of gooey green water—and they're starting to hiss and bubble! Just then, Kiran spots a drain on the other side of the room. It looks like you need to follow the arrows to find a safe route across the room, get to the drain, and flush the toxic water away.

SECURITY LEVEL 1

With the toxic goo water now safely flushed away, you head over to the exit following what's left of the green slime trail, only to find the door is locked. What next? Fortunately, with her keen eye for tech, Cassia spots a digital screen on the wall that flashes up a message.

PLEASE ANSWER
SECURITY LEVEL 1 QUESTION:

Which of the following plants is NOT carnivorous?

1. Flesh-eating cobra lily ☐

2. Rancid flytrap ☐

3. Tiger-tooth pitcher plant ☐

4. Spiky neon nut ☐

5. Ravenous monkey cup ☐

SECURITY LEVEL 2

You didn't think it was going to be that easy, did you?
Another message flashes up on the screen on the wall.

**PLEASE ANSWER
SECURITY LEVEL 2 QUESTION:**

Which of these plants is NOT a true flesh-eating cobra lily?

You have 30 seconds to answer.

◊ ECO FACT

Researchers brought to life a long-extinct plant, *Silene stenophylla*, using seeds buried by a squirrel 32,000 years ago. The ice-age seeds were found in a frozen riverbank in Siberia.

Your task is to spot the imposter plant in just 30 seconds. Are you and the team up to it?

They all look just the same to me! The difference must be tiny!

Suspect spotted

When Zane taps on the imposter, a loud click sounds as the door unlocks. Finally, you all run out of the Carnivorous Zone and into the next room ...

ROOM FOUR:
THE NURSERY

Great work, team! You've managed to lull a room full of flesh-eating plants to sleep AND save them from the toxic green slime. You've even used your new-found plant knowledge to pass some tricky security tests. It's all paid off, because now you are free to get back to the most important job—tracking down the source of the ghastly goo. And by the looks of things, you'd better hurry. The slime is multiplying at an alarming rate! It's literally everywhere—and there's a river of it oozing under the door of the nursery ahead.

This is where researchers nurture the seedlings of all the rare species, but what else lies in wait behind those doors? It's time to follow the oozing slime and find out ...

GET THE PICTURE?

Your first challenge is to figure out how to open the door to the nursery. On the wall is a screen displaying an image of a building in a grid. Next to it, there's a second grid, but the image is mixed up. To gain entry, you must put the pieces in the second grid in the right order to match the first.

That's a picture of the dome!

Ha! Ha! Ha!

What do you call a jungle where the animals talk about current events?

A topical rain forest!

Write the correct number or draw the correct piece in each square to solve the puzzle. Good luck!

Picture perfect!

With all the correct pieces in place, the doors in front of you glide open. You all rush hastily into the nursery ... and stop immediately!

SAVE THE SEEDS!

What on Earth has gone on in here? It looks like someone has left in a hurry. There are jars all over the floor and seeds scattered everywhere! Whatever you do, don't step on them—they could be really rare. Kiran instructs everyone to collect the seeds before the slime can damage them. Can you sort the seeds by coloring them in? You'll also need to check that there is the correct number of seeds as labeled on each jar.

43

THE HEAT IS ON

Like all the other labs, the nursery is deserted and the slime has been wreaking havoc in here too. It's oozed all over the control panels of the growing lamps for some rare seedlings and messed up the settings. You need to reset the temperatures for the lamps immediately or those seedlings could die! But how will you know what the correct temperature is? Luckily, Ethan notices a temperature chart on the wall with some instructions.

A

B

C

D

E

Love it! This is like doing my math homework!

⬧ ECO FACT

Earth has more than 80,000 species of edible plants, but 90 percent of the plant-based food we eat comes from just 30 plants.

Write the correct temperature in the box for each lamp.

Lamp	Temperature	
A	10 °C	10 °C
B	A + 5 °C	
C	B – 2 °C	
D	A + C	
E	D – B	

Under control!

As soon the team reset the lamps, the seedlings begin to perk up. You are just about to leave when Zane spots a suspicious-looking picture in a frame on the wall, with the words "*Periculum uligo*" underneath it.

PICTURE PERFECT

The specimen in the picture is so weird that Zane decides to make a quick sketch of it before you leave. He has a feeling it might be important in some way. Can you help Zane complete his sketch of the freaky plant? Don't leave out any details.

PERICULUM ULIGO

Hurry up Zane!
We need to get moving!

Genius!

Zane finishes up his sketch
and you leave the nursery.
It's time to find the source of
the slime before it does any
more damage!

47

ROOM FIVE:
THE TOP-SECRET LAB

Amazing work, team! You've rescued rare seeds and specimens from the green goo and solved tricky problems along the way—but there's still one major challenge to complete—and quickly! You MUST find the source of the toxic trail and put a stop to it. Right now, the goo is still contained within the building, but it won't be long before it leaks into the air vents. If that happens, there's nothing to stop it escaping into the outside world.

The good news is that you're getting close. The trail of slime has led you to a huge room labeled "Top Secret." This may be the place where the most dangerous experiments are carried out. There's slime from floor to ceiling and the smell is terrible, so hold your breath and let's go!

LAB LOCKDOWN

On the door to the laboratory is a leaf symbol. It looks just like the leaf symbols that Zane has been sketching along the way. Cassia quickly scans the symbol on the door with her tablet and a message appears on her screen: "Please select the correct leaf sequence to gain access to the lab. An incorrect entry will activate laboratory lockdown." That does not sound good. Can you identify the correct sequence?

1

2

3

ALL TIED UP!

The lab is overrun with tangled vines. What's more, there are people trapped inside, and boy, are they relieved to see you! You carefully make your way over to one of the captives—Professor Greenwood—and she explains that the team have been trapped there all night. The only way to release them is to relax the vines. The antidote you need is in one of the many bottles on the shelf, but unfortunately not all the flasks are labeled. That's no issue for you, though, as Professor Greenwood describes what to look for.

Two blue stripes

Yellow leaf symbol

Pink label

◊ ECO FACT

Bamboo is the fastest-growing woody plant in the world. It can grow nearly three feet (one meter) in a single day.

Listen up!

As Kiran applies the antidote, the professor explains that an experiment on a rare slime-producing plant went wrong. "We tried to stop it," she says, "but the slime took over. It made these vines grow out of control in moments! We have to stop it before it does any more damage!"

OPERATION ULIGO

The formula won't take effect for hours, so you must go on without the professor. She explains that you'll find the experiment in a lab along the corridor—look out for the sign on the door saying "Periculum Uligo." The antidote to the experiment-gone-wrong is in the cupboard there too, but beware—there'll be tricky security tests to pass! Unfortunately, the door signs have all been obliterated by green slime. Can you still work out which is the correct room?

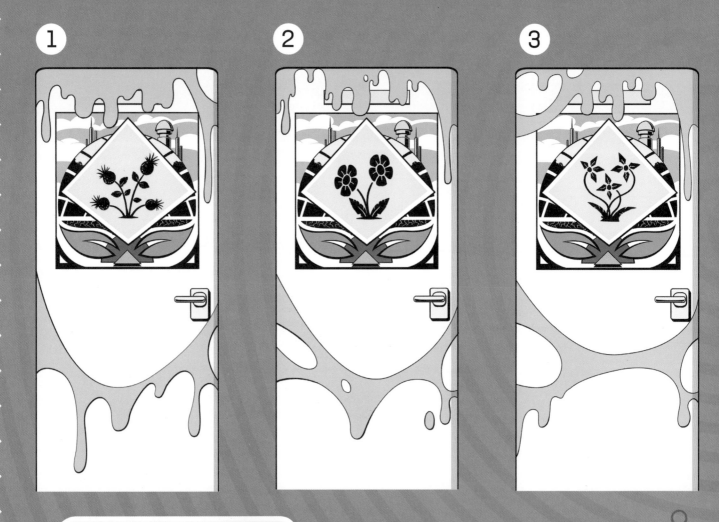

1 **2** **3**

🔥 ECO FACT

Scientists think they have identified two types of plant tough enough to survive on Mars—lichens and cyanobacteria. These were the first plants to colonize Earth 500 million years ago.

IDENTICAL RINGS

On a desk next to the cupboard, there's a computer.
Ethan quickly taps its keyboard and the screen wakes up.
A message appears, accompanied by a series of interlocking
rings with symbols on them.

**To gain access to the antidote store, please
complete the following security test:**

Which two rings have identical red
and white symbols on them?

Ha! Ha! Ha!

What kind of tree can
fit in your hand?
A palm tree!

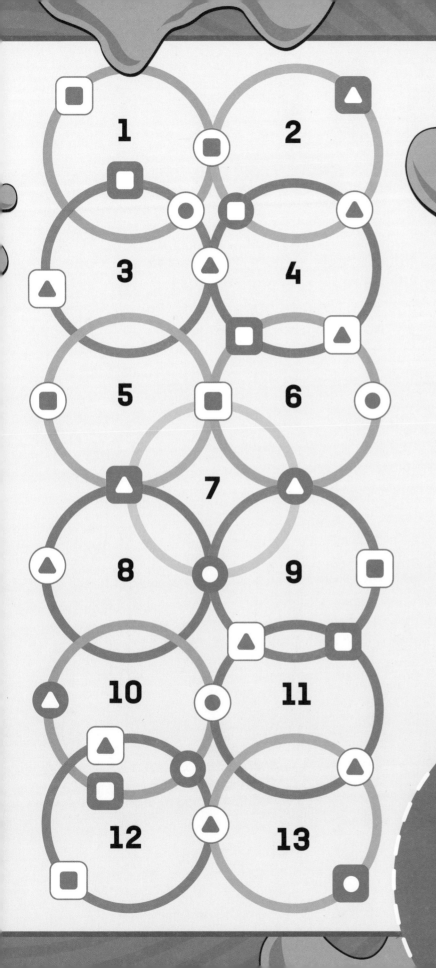

1

2

3

4

5

6

7

8

9

10

11

12

13

You did it!

As you click on the matching rings, the lock on the cupboard releases. It's time to put a stop to that slime once and for all!

FIND THE FORMULATION

Gingerly, Ethan opens the cabinet door. Inside, there's a rack holding four identical-looking test tubes with a note under each one. Only one of the tubes holds the correct formulation for the antidote, but which is it? Cassia quickly scans the symbol on the tubes and a message pops up on her screen. Look at page 59 to find out more.

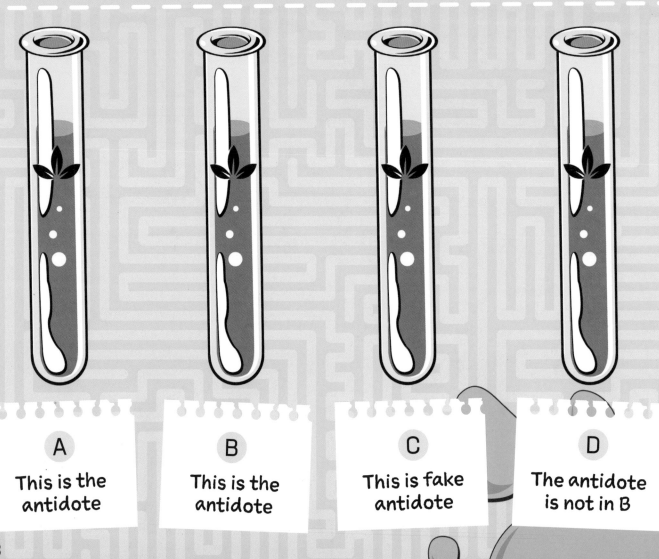

A
This is the antidote

B
This is the antidote

C
This is fake antidote

D
The antidote is not in B

If only one of these notes is true, which one contains the antidote?

If A is the true note, then all the others would need to be false ...

Work out your answer here!

The real antidote is:

Can't fool us!

Amazing! You have correctly identified the antidote. It's time to move on and wrap up this disaster!

TANK TROUBLE

You all charge into the final room and are met face-to-face with a bubbling, oozing slime monster—the plant experiment that went wrong! Even worse, it looks like it's about to break loose. You have the antidote in hand and there's no time to lose!

In front of you is a giant glass tank connected to five different watering systems. Only one leads to the slime monster. To control it, you'll have to drop the antidote into the correct tank that leads straight to the monster—but which one is that?

There's only one tube of antidote, so we only get one chance!

We can track the path of the water through the tubes and chambers to find the right one!

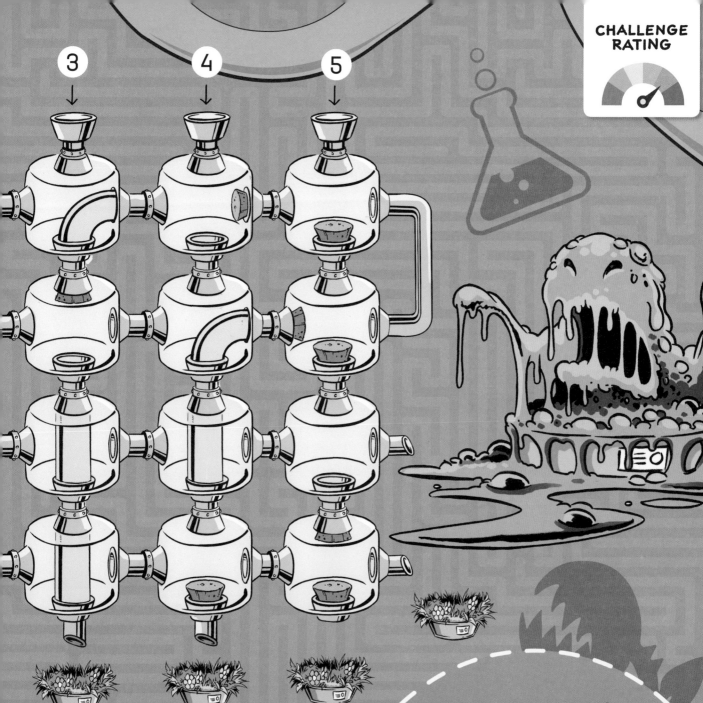

CHALLENGE RATING

3 4 5

You did it!

As the antidote takes effect, the slimy monster beings to shrivel, returning to it's normal plant state. The world is safe from toxic slime for now! You may have missed the official tour of the dome, but you've seen things that your classmates would never believe—and what's more, you've averted an eco-disaster!

Water can travel down the tubes ...

... or overflow into the next tank.

ANSWERS

PAGES 10-11
The answer is 2.

PAGES 12-13

PAGES 14-15
The answer is door 8.

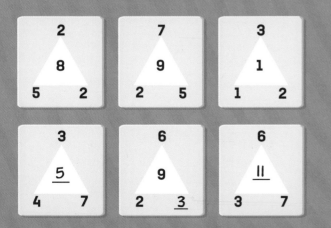

PAGES 18-19
The top and bottom left numbers are multiplied, then the bottom right number is subtracted.

2 / **8** / 5 2	**7** / **9** / 2 5	**3** / **1** / 1 2
3 / **5** / 4 7	**6** / **9** / 2 3	**6** / **11** / 3 7

PAGES 20-21
Giant prickly paw: 1
Thorny devil fruit: 3
Bristling bananas: 5
Spiky neon nut: 2
Ghost fingers: 4

PAGES 22-23
Fill vessel A with 9 cups of water, then empty it into vessel B twice, so that you are left with 1 cup of water in vessel A. Empty that into vessel B. That will leave room for 3 more cups of water in B. Fill up A again (9 cups), then use it to fill up B (3 cups). You will be left with 6 cups in vessel A.

PAGES 24-25

PAGES 28-29
The answer is 3. (Divide the top number by the middle number to get the answer.)

PAGES 30-31

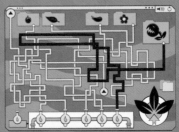

The answer is hose 5.

PAGES 32-33

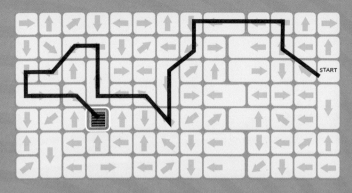

PAGES 34-35
The answer is 4,
spiky neon nut.

PAGES 36-37

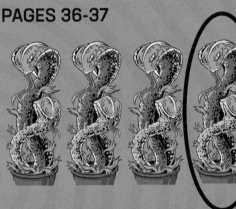

PAGES 40-41

14	7	1	12
2	10	4	5
11	8	15	13
9	6	16	3

PAGES 44-45
Lamp B: 15°c
Lamp C: 13°c
Lamp D: 23°c
Lamp E: 8°c

PAGES 50-51
The answer is 5.

PAGES 52-53

PAGES 54-55

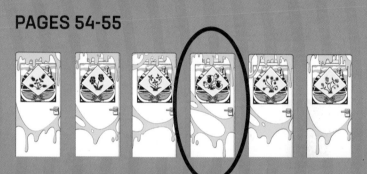

PAGES 56-57
The answer is circles 3 and 11.

PAGES 58-59
D is the only one that can be the
true statement—and if D is true, it
means that the other three must be
false, so C has to be the antidote.

PAGES 60-61
The answer is 2.

SEE YOU ON THE NEXT ADVENTURE!

Color in the team!